{ RECYCLED HOME }

←⊏ RECYCLED HOME ⊐→

TRANSFORM YOUR HOME USING SALVAGED MATERIALS

Rebecca Proctor

Laurence King Publishing

LAURENCE KING

Published in 2012 by
Laurence King Publishing Ltd
361–373 City Road
London EC1V 1LR
United Kingdom
Tel: + 44 20 7841 6900
Fax: +44 20 7841 6910

e-mail: enquiries@laurenceking.com
www.laurenceking.com

A catalogue record for this book is available
from the British Library.

ISBN: 978-1-85669-896-2

Illustrations by Andrew Wightman

Design: Bianca Wendt
Styling: Rebecca Proctor and Claire Walsh

Printed in China on Forest Stewardship Council
approved paper. www.fsc.org

FOR WREN

ACKNOWLEDGMENTS
Throughout the creation of this book I have
sought help and advice on the various projects
from several people. I am particularly indebted to
Andrew Wightman, Claire Walsh and Bette Proctor
for all their time, energy and ideas. Thank you!

ABOUT THE AUTHOR
Rebecca Proctor is a design writer with ten years'
experience in both the fashion and interiors
industries. She is particularly interested in all areas
relating to craft, craftsmanship and sustainable
design. Rebecca is the author of *1000 New Eco
Designs and Where to Find Them* and co-author of
New Shoes: Contemporary Footwear Design, both
published by Laurence King Publishing.

CONTENTS

—•—

—•—

⊰ LIVING ⊱
12

⊰ SLEEPING ⊱
40

⊰ BATHING ⊱
60

⊏- **DINING** -⊐
76

⊏· **UTILITY** ·⊐
94

⊏← **KIDS** →⊐
110

⊏-← **OUTDOOR** →-⊐
130

Introduction

Any recycling project begins with the thrill of the hunt.

For the committed crafter, almost everything has the potential to be transformed into something else. From rummaging through garage sales and flea markets to collecting washed-up wood at the beach, the joy is in discovering something unwanted and seeing what it could become. At that point – the point of discovery – the possibilities are limitless.

There are several reasons why we reuse materials: economy, resourcefulness, exclusivity, connection to the past, experimentation and play; but perhaps the most important reason is sustainability. It is not feasible for us to keep on consuming at the rate we do.

Everybody knows that we should reduce our footprint on the world, and getting down to some good old-fashioned making is one of the easiest ways to do it. When you realize that you need something, think first about how you could make it, rather than where you can buy it from; instead of shopping for gifts, craft them. Anyone with a heart would prefer a handmade gift to a shop-bought one, because they come with time, thought and love invested in them.

The purpose of this book is to show a range of projects all made from recycled and repurposed materials. Some are made entirely from scraps, while others combine new and old together. The projects are varied, ranging from sewing and knitting to woodwork and paper crafts. The aim is that everyone will find some inspiration among the pages regardless of their tastes and interests.

Many of the projects need not be followed exactly: the ideas could be used as a starting point for your own project, depending on the tools and materials you have at hand. Don't worry if things don't always turn out as you expect.

Just experiment, have fun and enjoy the results!

Materials

Useful materials are all around us, just waiting to be reused.
Most of the materials used in this book can easily be found
and repurposed – it is just a case of looking at the world with
an open and creative mind.

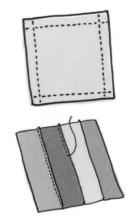

FABRIC We buy far too many clothes. It is one of
the saddest and most unnecessary habits of our
society. Inevitably they end up gathering dust at
the back of our wardrobes or, at best, get taken to
a charity store or fabric recycling bank. When you
are looking for fabric, the best place to start is by
looking at unwanted clothes. Are there any specific
colours or prints you are drawn to? Is there
enough fabric in that dress to make a pillowcase?
Even if there isn't, there will certainly be enough
for patchwork. Look at everything with fresh eyes
and you will see that your local charity shop is the
most wonderful fabric store in the world. Where
possible, choose natural fibres such as cotton,
linen and wool; not only are these fabrics easier to
wash and sew, but they will last much longer, too.

YARN There is no need to buy new yarn for a
knitting project. Unravel old sweaters and remove
the kinks by soaking in water. Alternatively, use up
odds and ends of wool or make patchwork from
tension squares.

TRIMS AND NOTIONS Buttons, zips, elastic
and so on can all be salvaged from unwanted
clothes. Even if the fabric is not to your liking,
consider what else could be reused. Nothing
need be wasted.

PAPER Cards, gift wrap, newspapers,
magazines and packaging are all sources of
wonderful imagery. Save your favourites and
reuse them at a later date.

SCRAP WOOD Old furniture, fallen branches,
driftwood and wood off-cuts all have the
potential to become useful materials. If you
have space, start a woodpile where you can
store all your finds.

Tools

Here is a selection of the most useful tools used to make the projects in this book. There is no need to buy all of them; build your toolbox slowly, along with your skills and interests. Take care of your tools: look after them and they will look after you!

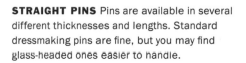

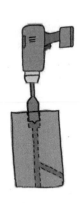

SEWING MACHINE A sewing machine is not absolutely essential, but it does make sewing quicker. There is no need for lots of fancy stitches; a very basic model is all that is required for the projects in this book.

HAND-SEWING NEEDLE This is one of the simplest and most useful tools available. There are lots of different types and it is well worth keeping a selection in your kit.

IRON AND IRONING BOARD Pressing fabric is an integral part of the sewing process. Creases need to be wrinkled out, folds pressed in and seams opened flat. There is no need to use a professional steam iron; a standard domestic one will work just fine.

FABRIC SCISSORS Save these sharp shears for cutting fabric only. Paper will blunt the blades.

PAPER SCISSORS Use ordinary stationery scissors for cutting paper.

PINKING SHEARS These have zigzag blades and are used to prevent seams and raw edges from fraying. They are by no means essential, but they do help to create a neat finish.

TAPE MEASURE A flexible tape measure is invaluable for all manner of projects.

TRANSPARENT PLASTIC RULER A transparent ruler allows you to see work while drawing straight lines.

METRE RULE (YARD STICK) This is useful for marking and measuring larger items.

STRAIGHT PINS Pins are available in several different thicknesses and lengths. Standard dressmaking pins are fine, but you may find glass-headed ones easier to handle.

SAFETY PINS Useful in any toolbox.

TAILOR'S CHALK Use this to mark cutting and sewing lines on fabric. The chalk lines are removable; simply brush them away.

DISAPPEARING-INK FABRIC PEN Used like tailor's chalk, but the ink disappears in 48 hours.

MARKER PEN An ordinary marker pen can be used for making stencils and drawing templates.

SEAM RIPPER Unpicks stitches and seams.

ROTARY CUTTER A quilting tool used for cutting multiple layers of fabric to the same length. Always use it with a cutting mat.

CUTTING MAT A protective rubber mat with a grid for precise measuring and cutting.

CRAFT KNIFE A sharp knife with replaceable blades in snap-off sections is a useful tool.

LOOP TURNER A fine metal wire that slips easily into narrow tubing to pull fabric the right side out.

HAMMER For driving and removing nails.

SAW The sharper the saw, the better.

DRILL This is essential for creating holes and driving screws.

⊰ LIVING ⊱

Patchwork tweed blanket - Book wallpaper - Feature cushion
Handmade lampshade - Scrapbook album - Papier mâché bowl
Roller crate - Scrap-wood picture frame - Fabric-wrapped notebook
Recycled storage cans - Furoshiki gift bag

Patchwork tweed blanket

This blanket is made from an assortment of old clothes, leftover fabric and samples of Harris tweed picked up on a visit to the Hebrides, off the coast of Scotland. The use of the tweed results in a beautiful, warm blanket full of holiday memories.

Time needed: A long weekend.

You will need:	Iron and board	Pinking shears
Fabric	Measuring tape	Sewing machine
Fabric scissors	Needle and thread	Straight pins

1

Select contrasting fabric of the same weight. The idea is to use up rags and unwanted pieces of fabric, so old clothes and scraps are ideal.

2

Wash, dry and press all fabric before you begin.

3

This blanket is made up of patchwork strips 15, 20 and 25cm (6, 8 and 10in) wide. Each strip is 150cm (59in) long. You need four strips of each width.

4

To make a 15cm (6in) wide strip, cut pieces of fabric that width, or that will add up to 15cm (6in) when joined. When joining smaller pieces, add on a seam allowance of 1cm (⅜in) for each join. For example, if you are joining three pieces together, two will need to be 6cm (2½in) wide and one 7cm (2¾in) wide to allow a seam on each side.

5

Once you have cut the fabric, pin together with the right sides facing.

6

Sew together using a 1cm (⅜in) seam allowance. Use tailor's chalk to mark the sewing line if this helps you sew a straighter line.

7

Now press the seams open and trim any excess with pinking shears to prevent fraying.

8

Using a 1cm (⅜in) seam allowance as before, join these pieces together by their long edges until you have a strip 150cm (59in) in length.

9

Repeat this process, cutting, stitching and pressing until you have 12 150cm (59in) strips.

10

Join six strips by pinning the right sides together and stitching a seam along the length of each strip. Again, use a 1cm (⅜in) seam allowance.

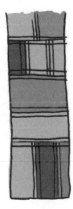

8

4

Patchwork tweed blanket

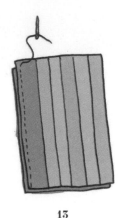

13

TIP

Patchwork doesn't have to follow a formula – vary the pattern as much or as little as you like.

-11-
Press the seams open and trim any excess with pinking shears to prevent fraying.

-12-
Repeat steps 10 and 11 with the remaining six strips.

-13-
Lay out the large pieces of patchwork, wrong sides together, and pin and baste all around the edges.

-14-
Machine-stitch around the entire blanket, using a 1cm (³⁄₈in) seam allowance.

-15-
To make the binding for the edge, cut various pieces of fabric 15cm (6in) wide by any length, and sew together end-to-end with a 1cm (³⁄₈in) seam allowance.

-16-
Press the seams open and trim with pinking shears.

-17-
With the wrong side facing up, fold in the two long edges by 2cm (³⁄₄in), towards the centre of the fabric. Press in place.

-18-
Pin the binding, wrong side to right side of blanket, along two opposite edges of the blanket.

-19-
Machine-stitch in place, making sure to catch the top and bottom of the binding as you go.

-20-
Repeat steps 18 and 19 for the other two edges of the blanket.

-21-
Press the blanket and remove any loose threads.

-22-
Finally, hand-sew the top and bottom together with small stitches at random. These can be as decorative or discreet as you like.

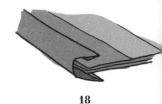

18

TIP

➤➤➤ Anthologies, poetry and short stories work particularly well, as you can dip in and out, reading a single page at a glance.

Book wallpaper

This is a great way to make the most of one of your favourite books. Chopping it up might seem like sacrilege at first, but having all the pages on one wall means you will see it every day instead of just occasionally.

Time needed: It will depend on the size of the wall, but this project is quicker than it looks. A small wall can easily be completed In an afternoon.

You will need:

Brush	Craft knife	Sponge
Book	Cutting mat	Wallpaper paste
Clean cloths	Hot soapy water	
	Ruler	

2

3

5

(1)
Before you start, make sure the wall is clean and dry.

(2)
Neatly cut pages from your book with a craft knife or scalpel. Once they are cut, neaten the inside edge again, if necessary.

(3)
Place a few pages face down on a flat work surface and brush lightly with wallpaper paste.

(4)
Starting in the top left corner of the wall, position the first page gently on the wall and ease into place.

(5)
Using a dry cloth, smooth over the paper horizontally to remove any wrinkles.

(6)
Repeat with the next page, first placing it on the wall, then gently smoothing out any wrinkles. Make sure the two pages line up neatly on the wall.

(7)
Clean any wallpaper paste off the work surface as you go. It is important to keep the work surface clean and dry between each pasting to avoid spoiling the right side of the pages.

(8)
To cut around a light switch, hold the page in position over it and press against the switch. Now cut a hole for the switch using the marks as guides.

6

(9)
When you reach the end of the wall, hold the unpasted pages In position and mark with a pencil where they need to be trimmed. Cut along the lines, paste and fix in place.

7

(10)
Repeat steps 5 and 6 until the wall is complete.

Feature cushion

Scatter cushions (throw pillows) are a great way to make a feature out of small pieces of vintage fabric. For a professional touch, finish your cushion with a zipper.

Time needed: One to two hours per cushion

You will need:

Cushion or pillow pad
Fabric
Fabric scissors

Iron and board
Seam ripper
Sewing machine with
zipper foot

Straight pins
Tape measure
Thread
Zipper

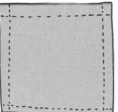

1

3

Cut two pieces of fabric the size of your cushion inner pad plus 2cm (¾in) all round. For example, if your cushion is 45 x 45cm (17¾ x 17¾in), your fabric will need to be 47 x 47cm (18½ x 18½in). This allows a 1cm (⅜in) seam allowance on all seams.

Place both pieces of fabric together with the right sides facing and all corners aligned.

Centre the zipper along what will be the bottom edge of the cushion and place a pin near each end of the zipper, just inside the metal stops.

With a 1cm (⅜in) seam allowance, sew the two short spaces on the outside edge of each pin. Reinforce the seams by back stitching at the beginning and end of each seam.

Change the stitch length on your machine to the longest length and baste the gap between the two short seams just made.

Press the seam open.

With the wrong side of the fabric facing up, place the zipper right side down, aligning the teeth directly over the seam. Pin in place.

Change the sewing machine's presser foot to the zipper foot. Consult your manual for help with this if necessary.

Making sure that the stitch length is back to normal length for the remainder of the sewing, start at the bottom of the zipper on the right side, with the zipper foot in the right-side position, and sew down the side of the zipper. Stop the machine just before the end and, leaving the needle in the work, raise the foot and gently move the zipper pull back behind the needle. Lower the foot again and sew to the end of the zipper. Backstitch at the end of this seam.

Change the zipper foot to the left position, and repeat this process on the left.

5

7

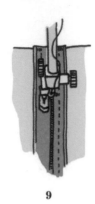

9

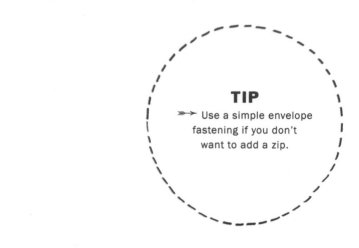

TIP
⟫→ Use a simple envelope
fastening if you don't
want to add a zip.

〔-11-〕
**Use the seam ripper to gently remove the
basted stitches.**

〔-12-〕
**Change back to the standard presser foot.
Fold the two halves of the cushion so they
are aligned with right sides facing each
other and all corners and edges lined up.
Pin in place.**

〔-13-〕
**Sew around the remaining three sides with
a 1cm (⅜in) seam allowance.**

〔-14-〕
**Remove the excess fabric at the corners
diagonally.**

〔-15-〕
**Turn right side out, pressing the seams flat,
and insert the cushion pad.**

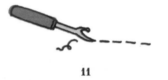

11

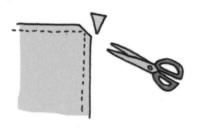

14

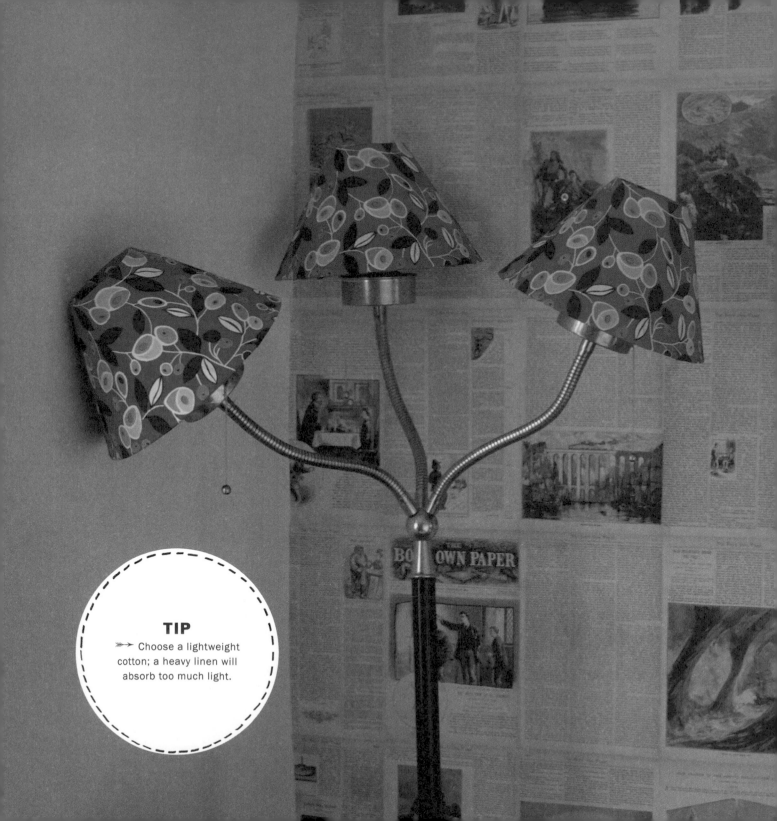

TIP

⟫ Choose a lightweight cotton; a heavy linen will absorb too much light.

Handmade lampshade

Old lampshades can easily be transformed by covering
the existing shade in new fabric.

Time needed: 30 minutes

You will need:
Clothes pegs
(clothespins)
Fabric

Fabric scissors
Lampshade
Masking tape
Paper

Paper scissors
Pen or pencil
Plastic sheet
Spray adhesive

5

7

8

(-1-)
Press the fabric.

(-2-)
Place a large sheet of paper on a work surface.

(-3-)
Use masking tape to stick the edge of
the paper onto the seam at the side of
the lampshade.

(-4-)
Starting at the seam, mark the shape of the top
and bottom edges of the shade onto the paper.

(-5-)
Carefully roll the shade along the paper,
continuing to draw the shape of the top
and bottom of the shade onto the paper.
Stop when you reach the seam again.

(-6-)
Remove the shade from the paper.

(-7-)
Adding 2cm (¾in) at the top and bottom,
cut the pattern from the paper. Check your
template is accurate by fitting it on the
shade and adjust if necessary.

(-8-)
Place the fabric right-side down on the work
surface. Pin the pattern to the fabric and
cut out.

(-9-)
Test-fit the fabric on the shade and trim
if necessary.

(-10-)
Cover the work surface with a plastic sheet
or other protective covering and, following
the manufacturer's instructions, spray the
back of the fabric with spray adhesive.

(-11-)
Beginning at the seam, lay the shade on one
edge of the fabric and carefully roll it onto
the fabric.

(-12-)
Pick up the shade and continue pressing
down the fabric, lightly stretching and
smoothing until the whole shade is covered.

(-13-)
Make a small clip every 2cm (¾in) into the
overhanging fabric at the top and bottom
of the shade. Fold this over and stick the
fabric onto the inside of the shade.

(-14-)
Hold in place with clothes pegs until the
adhesive is dry.

14

Scrapbook album

Good photo albums are surprisingly hard to find.
An interesting and more thoughtful alternative is to make
a bespoke album from an old hardback book.

Time needed: As long or as little as you like – this could be an ongoing project.

You will need:
Book
Paint, pens, brushes,
stickers and so on

Photographs
Photo corners

1

1
Choose a hardback book with strong pages. Browse old bookshops for the perfect album. Try to find one with an interesting or relevant subject matter, as you will still see parts of the cover and pages behind your photos.

2
Arrange photos on the pages and mount with photo corners.

3
Add customized embellishments with paint, pens, stickers and so on. The only limit is your imagination!

2

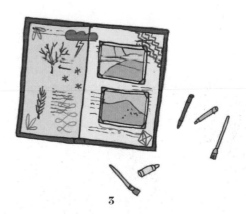

3

Papier mâché bowl

Everybody remembers making papier mâché when they were younger. This (slightly) more grown-up version is just as easy, and is a great project to do with children.

Time needed: Two hours plus drying time

You will need:
Bowls for moulds
Decorative paper
Newspaper
Paper scissors
Petroleum jelly
PVA glue (all-purpose white glue)
Varnish

8

1

Smear a layer of petroleum jelly all over the inside and edge of the bowl you are using for a mould. Make sure not to miss any spots.

2

Cut the newspaper into strips about 2cm (¾in) wide. You will need enough to cover the bowl completely in about ten layers.

3

Pour the glue into a dish and water it down slightly. The ratio should be one part water to three parts glue.

4

Start the first layer of papier mâché by dipping a strip of paper in the glue mixture then laying it inside the bowl. Continue until the whole bowl is covered, overlapping the pieces as you go.

5

Keep building up layer upon layer of papier mâché, making sure that the pieces lay flat without any bubbling.

5

6

When you have applied ten layers, leave the bowl to dry overnight.

7

Once the bowl is dry, gently pull the bowl out of the bowl mould.

8

Use scissors to neaten the rim of the bowl.

9

Now apply the decorative inner and outer layers of the bowl by repeating steps 2–4 with your chosen paper. This time, use triangle-shaped pieces of paper to help cover the bowl neatly. Also, wrap pieces up and over the edge for a smooth rim.

9

10

Leave to dry for a few hours, then coat the bowl with varnish to seal. Allow to dry completely.

10

TIP

➤ Use castors with brakes
to stop your box
rolling away.

Roller crate

This is an easy way to transform a humble wooden box into a fun and practical mobile storage unit.

Time needed: 30 minutes

You will need:
Castors
Drill
Pencil
Sandpaper
Screws
Wooden crate

1

Check that your box is clean and remove any rough edges with sandpaper.

Turn the box upside down and place one castor on each corner.

Make pencil marks on the box through the screw holes on the castors.

Remove the castors and drill holes for the screws through the pencil marks.

Place the castors on the box again and screw firmly into place.

3

4

5

OISEAUX

Scrap-wood picture frame

Embrace the imperfections of scrap wood by transforming it into simple picture frames.

Time needed: One to two hours

You will need:

Cardboard	Mitre box	Saw
Craft knife	Panel pins	Scrap wood
Hammer	Pencil	Vice
Metal ruler	Picture glass	Wood glue
	Sandpaper	

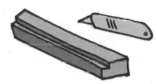

Source pieces of wood with character that are of a pleasing width to frame your picture.

Decide what size you want the window of your frame to be. It should be about 5mm (¼in) smaller than the size of your picture so that the frame covers the edges.

If you want the viewing window to be 19 x 9cm (7½ x 3½in), for a picture sized 20 x 10cm (8 x 4in), you will need enough wood to make two sides slightly longer than 19cm (7½in) and two sides slightly longer than 9cm (3½in). The extra length allows room for cutting mitres at each end. This creates a neat finish, which will provide a pleasing contrast to the patina of the scrap wood.

Mark the exact length of each side of the window onto each piece of wood with a ruler and pencil. Roughly cut the four sides of your frame, remembering to allow some extra length for the mitres.

Make cuts at 45 degrees outwards from these marks using your mitre box. Once you have cut all four sides, make sure that both horizontal pieces and both vertical pieces are identical in size.

Now make a notch along the edge of each piece where the glass and picture will sit. Clamping each piece into the vice, make a cut along its edge, then turn it 90 degrees and make another cut so a strip of wood is removed. Be careful to make each cut the same distance in from the edge so the glass will fit tightly.

Glue the four corners together and hold in place. Once dry, gently smooth any rough edges with a piece of sandpaper.

Fit your glass and picture in the frame, adding a piece of cardboard at the back for protection. Fix gently in place with panel pins, and the frame is complete.

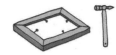

Fabric-wrapped notebook

This project turns an ordinary inexpensive notebook into a treasured gift. It is also a great way to use up leftover pieces of favourite fabric.

Time needed: 30 minutes plus drying time

You will need:
Fabric
Hardback notebook
Plastic bag
PVA glue (all-purpose white glue)
Sandpaper
Scissors
Sugar paper (construction paper)

⊂1⊃
Choose a lightweight cotton fabric. If the fabric is too heavy, the corners will be bulky; if it is too light, the glue will show through. Lawn cotton is ideal. Press the fabric.

⊂2⊃
Lightly sand the cover of the notebook to help the fabric adhere to it.

⊂3⊃
Measure the amount of fabric you need. Place the book, opened out, on top of the fabric and allow an extra 2.5cm (1in) all around. Cut out.

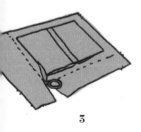

3

⊂4⊃
Cut out two pieces of sugar paper. They should be about 5mm (¼in) smaller on all sides than the book's cover. Put aside.

⊂5⊃
Lay the book flat and place centrally on the fabric, keeping the 2.5cm (1in) allowance all around. Lift the cover, brush with glue, and press flat onto the fabric again.

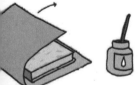

5

⊂6⊃
Brush glue on the back and the spine and press these down again.

⊂7⊃
Smooth out any wrinkles, paying particular attention to the spine.

⊂8⊃
Open up the book and make two snips into the 2.5cm (1in) allowance at the spine. Repeat this at both ends of the spine.

8

⊂9⊃
Make cuts at each corner, taking off a small triangle of fabric.

⊂10⊃
Glue and fold over the edges.

⊂11⊃
Brush glue on the sugar paper and stick a piece inside the front and back covers of the book, covering the fabric edges. Close the book and press shut, placing a plastic bag between the covers and the pages to protect the pages from glue.

9

⊂12⊃
Neaten the spine by opening and pulling back the book covers. Using scissors, poke the remaining fabric down the spine, being careful not to get glue on the pages.

Recycled storage cans

Upcycle empty tin cans and scraps of paper by making these useful storage containers.

Time needed: 30 minutes

You will need:

Craft knife
Decorative paper
Empty food cans

Measuring tape
PVA glue (all-purpose white glue)
Ruler

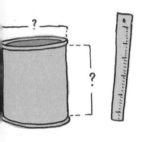

2

 1

Open the cans carefully leaving the rim in place as shown. This will help keep the paper in place. Remove any wrapping from the can. Wash thoroughly and leave to dry.

 2

Measure the height of the can between the top and bottom ridges and the diameter across the top.

 3

Multiply the diameter by 3.5 to give you the length of your paper strip plus a small overlap.

 4

Cut out a paper strip neatly with a craft knife to the right measurements.

 5

Test-fit the paper around the can, making any necessary adjustments.

 6

Apply a line of glue along the end of the strip, wrap it around the can, and hold in place until dry.

4

5

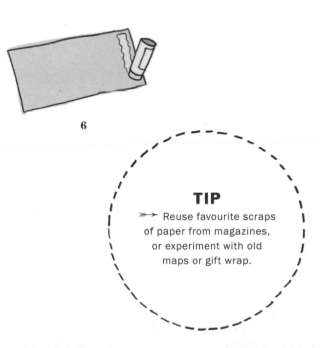

6

TIP

⇒ Reuse favourite scraps of paper from magazines, or experiment with old maps or gift wrap.

Furoshiki gift bag

Furoshiki is a traditional Japanese wrapping cloth that is used to transport food, clothes and gifts – almost anything, in fact. As the cloths are reusable, they make the perfect sustainable gift wrap and spell the end to piles of unwanted wrapping paper.

Time needed: 30 minutes

You will need:
Fabric
Fabric scissors
Iron and board

Measuring tape
Needle and thread
Straight pins

1
Cut and hem a 50 x 50cm (20 x 20in) square of fabric (or bigger or smaller, depending on the size of your gift).

2
With the right side of the fabric facing down, place the gift in the centre of the square.

3
Bring one of the corners up and over the gift, covering the item and tucking the corner underneath.

4
Bring the opposite corner up and over, securing the gift snugly.

5
Now bring the remaining two corners together and tie in a knot.

2

3

4

5

TIP
⟫→ This is a basic wrap, but there are dozens of different ways to tie Furoshiki. Search online for more to learn.

(- SLEEPING -)

Vintage pillowcases - Woodland log light
Warm winter eiderdown - Recycled blind - Braided rag rug
Cosy hot water bottle cover - Night owl lavender cushion

Vintage pillowcases

Beautiful bedlinen can transform a bedroom, yet it is often prohibitively expensive. However, vintage-fabric pillowcases are easy to make and add a unique feel to your room.

Time needed: Two hours

You will need:
Fabric
Fabric scissors
Iron and board
Measuring tape
Needle and thread
Pinking shears
Straight pins

(- 1 -)
Cut a piece of fabric measuring 180cm wide by 53cm long (71 x 21in). This will make one pillowcase with a closure flap at one end.

(- 2 -)
Turn under a double 1.2cm (½in) hem at one end of the fabric. Stitch and press.

2

(- 3 -)
At the opposite end, turn under a double 5cm (2in) hem. Stitch and press.

(- 4 -)
Place the fabric on a flat surface, right side up, and mark a line with pins 15cm (6in) from the end with the small hem.

(- 5 -)
Fold the end with the large hem to this mark and pin the side seams, 1.2cm (½in) in from the raw edge.

5

(- 6 -)
Fold the end with the small hem over the top at the line of pins.

(- 7 -)
Pin the side seams 1.2cm (½in) in from the raw edges.

(- 8 -)
Stitch both side seams through all thicknesses.

(- 9 -)
Press open and trim the excess with pinking shears.

(- 10 -)
Turn right side out and press.

(- 11 -)
Put the pillow in the pillowcase and tuck it under the flap to secure.

6

Woodland log light

Bring the magic of the forest into your home with
a sylvan table lamp.

Time needed: 1 hour 30 minutes

You will need:	Lampshade	Sandpaper
Drill	Lamp holder with	Saw
Drill bit	a screw-in base	
Electrical flex with plug	Log	

(- 1 -)

Choose a well-seasoned hardwood log with
firm bark.

(- 2 -)

Decide how tall the lamp base will be. Bear
in mind that the height of the base cannot
be more than twice the length of the drill
bit, as you will need to drill all the way
through the centre of the base.

(- 3 -)

Saw the log straight at both ends to make
a level top and base.

(- 4 -)

Drill through the centre of the log from top
to bottom. You may need to drill in from
either end and meet in the middle. Make
sure that the hole is wide enough to
accommodate the electrical flex.

(- 5 -)

Drill another hole at 45 degrees through the
bark, 3cm (1¼in) from the base, to meet
the vertical hole. This is where the electrical
flex will pass through.

(- 6 -)

With a larger drill bit, increase the size
of the hole at the top of the lamp base
to accommodate the screw fitting of the
lamp holder.

(- 7 -)

Sand the top and bottom of the base
until smooth.

(- 8 -)

Feed the electrical flex through the side
hole and out through the top. Stick a pencil
through the bottom hole to help poke it
through.

(- 9 -)

Wire the flex into the lamp holder.
If you are unsure about this, consult
an electrician.

(- 10 -)

Screw the lamp holder into the base and fit
the lampshade.

6

8

Warm winter eiderdown

Traditional eiderdowns were stuffed with the feathers of the eider, a large Arctic duck. This version updates the old classic by using an unwanted duvet (comforter) instead. Topped with handprinted fabric with a vintage-sheet back, the eiderdown is also reversible.

Time needed: Two hours

You will need:

Bodkin	Fabric scissors	Needle and thread	Thimble
Duvet (comforter)	Iron and board	Sewing machine	
Fabric	Measuring tape	Silk thread	
	Needle grabber or pliers	Straight pins	

(- 1 -)

Cut two pieces of fabric 100 x 125cm (39½ x 49¼in).

(- 2 -)

With the two right sides together, pin and stitch a 1cm (⅜in) seam along all four sides, leaving a 30cm (12in) gap on one side.

(- 3 -)

Turn inside out.

(- 4 -)

Press seams flat.

(- 5 -)

Cut the duvet to 100 x 125cm (39½ x 49¼in) in size. Pin the cut edge and stitch together. If you are using a feather duvet, be careful not to lose too many feathers!

(- 6 -)

Insert the duvet into the eiderdown cover and handstitch the gap closed.

(- 7 -)

Using scraps of leftover fabric, cut 18 squares that are 2 x 2cm (¾ x ¾in).

(- 8 -)

Pin the squares onto the reverse of the eiderdown in an offset grid formation.

(- 9 -)

Using the bodkin, pull the silk thread through the centre of each square, joining the front, back and middle layers together. If you are using a feather-filled duvet, this will be quite stiff; you may need to use a needle grabber or pliers to pull the bodkin through.

(- 10 -)

Secure with a knot and leave a tassel for decoration.

2

6

9

10

Recycled blind

Roman blinds make a stylish and simple window covering. Although they are expensive to buy, they are surprisingly easy to make and require very little sewing skill. This blind was made using fabric left over from an upholstery project.

Time needed: Five hours

You will need:

Fabric	Iron and board	a rail system, fibreglass rods,
Fabric scissors	Lining fabric	tape, cord drops and brackets
Hacksaw	Measuring tape	Sewing machine
	Roman blind kit including	Straight pins

4

Allowance for cord

2

finished length

(- 1 -)
Decide what size you want your finished blind to be.

(- 2 -)
To calculate the size of your pleats, deduct an allowance for the track and cord lock of 6cm (2½in). Divide the remaining number by an odd number to find the size of the pleat sections, which should be approximately 10–20cm (4–8in) long. For example, finished blind length is 86cm, – 6cm = 80cm to pleat. 80cm ÷ 5 pleat sections = 16cm folds (finished blind length is 34in, – 2½in = 31½in to pleat. 31½in ÷ 5 pleat sections = 6⅓in folds). The rods fall between sections 2 & 3 and 4 & 5 and the folds on the front of the blind fall between 1 & 2 and 3 & 4. The alternative to having five pleat sections is either three larger sections with one rod pocket or seven smaller sections with three rod pockets.

(- 3 -)
Cut the fabric to the finished size of the blind, adding 5cm (2in) to each side, the top and bottom for turning allowances.

(- 4 -)
On the right side of the fabric, mark with pins the 5cm (2in) side and bottom turning allowances. Place a pin in each corner point.

(- 5 -)
Lay the fabric on a table, right side down. Turn in the sides, hem 5cm (2in) and pin in place. Turn each corner up 45 degrees so that the fold runs through the corner pin. Turn up 5cm (2in) to make the mitred corners and pin in place. Trim away the excess fabric in the corner of the mitre.

(- 6 -)
Cut out the lining fabric to the finished width of the blind and add 5cm (2in) to the length of the blind. Fold and press in 2.5cm (1in) down the sides and 2.5cm (1in) along the lower edge of the lining.

5

(- 7 -)
Temporarily pin the lining into position on the back of the blind 2.5cm (1in) in from each side and 2.5cm (1in) up from the hem fold.

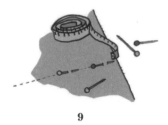

9

10

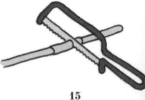

15

(- 8 -)
Calculate the rod pocket positions by
following step 2.

(- 9 -)
Mark the horizontal lines of the tape
positions on the lining with a row of pins.
Remove the lining from the blind fabric.

(- 10 -)
Cut the tapes the width of the blind and
place onto the marked lines. Make sure the
open slits for the fibreglass rods face the
top of the blind. Turn the ends of the tape
in 2cm (¾in) to close and neaten. Either
hand-sew or machine-stitch in place on the
lower edge of the tape. Hand-sew the ends
of the tape to neaten.

(- 11 -)
Reposition the lining on the back of the blind
2.5cm (1in) in from the sides and 2.5cm
(1in) up from the hem fold. Slipstitch down
each side and along the hem, taking care not
to stitch through to the front of the blind.

(- 12 -)
To hold the lining to the fabric, hand-sew
small spot tack stitches through the fabrics
just below the rod pocket tapes. These will
be barely visible from the front and ensure
that the blind will hang neatly.

(- 13 -)
To make the top hem, measure the finished
length up from the bottom and mark
horizontally with a row of pins. Fold the
fabric over the pin line.

(- 14 -)
Machine-sew the loop tape onto the back of
the blind along the top edge only. Trim away
the excess fabric and machine-stitch the
lower edge and ends of the tape.

(- 15 -)
Cut the required number of fibreglass rods
to the length of the sewn rod pocket tape
less 1cm (⅜in). Wear protective gloves,
as fibreglass splinters. Wrap tape around the
cutting area and then cut with a hacksaw.
Fit the protective end caps and slip the rods
into the rod pocket tape, through the slits at
the top of the tape.

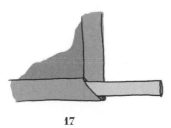

17

(- 16 -)
Cut the flat aluminium bar to the width
of the blind less 2cm (¾in). Fit the plastic
end caps at each end to prevent snagging
the fabric.

(- 17 -)
Slip the bar through the mitres at the hem
of the blind and handstitch to enclose.

(- 18 -)
To fit the blind to the track, press the
loop tape on the blind to the hook tape
on the track.

(- 19 -)
Thread the cord directly through the slits
in the rod pocket tape.

(- 20 -)
Tie the cords onto the lowest rod pocket
tape and trap the cords through the
locking device.

(- 21 -)
Trim the cords to within 10cm (4in) to allow
for adjustment.

(- 22 -)
Ensure all cords are equally tensioned and,
with the blind lying flat, tie the cords
together and trim the ends 15cm (6in)
below the cord lock.

(- 23 -)
Clip the blind onto the brackets and adjust
the cord tensions if necessary.

20

22

Braided rag rug

Like patchwork quilts, braided rugs are a classic piece of early American colonial culture. Made from scraps of old clothing, braided and then coiled together, each rug is filled with history and tells a story about its past.

Time needed: Depends how long you want to take – could be a weekend or a whole winter!

You will need:
Bodkin
Fabric
Fabric scissors
Iron and board
Pinking shears
Strong thread

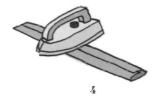

4

5

(– 1 –)
Choose the fabric carefully, making sure that it is all of a similar weight. This rug was made using medium-weight wools and includes a mixture of old suiting, flannel shirts and various other items.

(– 2 –)
Wash, dry and press all the fabric.

(– 3 –)
Cut into strips 3cm (1¼in) wide and as long as possible.

(– 4 –)
Iron the strips and fold 1cm (⅜in) in from the two edges, creating one strip 1cm (⅜in) wide. Press.

(– 5 –)
Take three pieces of varying lengths and sew together securely at one end.

(– 6 –)
Braid the three pieces together, holding the end between your toes.

6

Braided rag rug

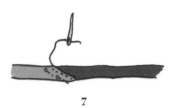

7

(- 7 -)
When you reach the end of one piece, attach another by pinning and stitching it to the end. If you sew diagonally, you will create a neater finish.

(- 8 -)
Trim any excess fabric at the join with pinking shears.

(- 9 -)
Continue braiding. Don't worry if the join is not perfect, as it will be hidden and strengthened by the braid.

(- 10 -)
Continue braiding until all the fabric strips have been used.

(- 11 -)
Secure the end by stitching then binding tightly together.

(- 12 -)
To begin shaping the rug, take one end of the braid and fold it over on itself by 10cm (4in).

(- 13 -)
Take the thread and tie it into the middle of the end of the braid.

(- 14 -)
Working from the middle of the braid to the middle of the braid, use the bodkin to pull the thread through and stitch together the folded-over pieces. You aren't passing through any fabric, simply through the holes between the plaits.

(- 15 -)
Continue like this, winding the braid around and around and stitching securely in place. To make sure that the rug lies flat, be careful not to pull the stitches too tight. Keep checking as you go.

(- 16 -)
At the end, stitch through the centre of the fabric strips, pass the thread through the middle of the plait, and secure in place.

11

14

Cosy hot water bottle cover

A hot water bottle is a joy on cold winter nights. These covers are made from an old Welsh tapestry blanket, but any other woollen material such as an old sweater would work just as well.

1

Time needed: One hour

You will need:
Fabric
Fabric scissors
Tracing paper

Hot water bottle
Iron and board
Marker pen
Needle and thread

Pinking shears
Straight pins

5

(- 1 -)
Place the hot water bottle on the tracing paper and, adding an extra 2cm (¾in) all over, draw around the edge.

(- 2 -)
Cut out and pin to the fabric.

(- 3 -)
Cut a piece of fabric this size.

(- 4 -)
Cut another piece of fabric the same shape but 10cm (4in) longer.

(- 5 -)
Cut the second piece of fabric horizontally to make two pieces – a small piece for the top and a larger piece for the bottom. When they are placed together they will overlap.

(- 6 -)
Fold, press and pin a hem on both of the overlapping edges. Stitch.

(- 7 -)
Lay the larger cut piece right side up, and place the smaller piece on top, right side down. Then put the first piece you cut on top, also right side down. Make sure the hems of the two cut pieces are overlapping.

(- 8 -)
Pin together and sew carefully around all edges.

(- 9 -)
Press open the seam and trim any excess with pinking shears.

(- 10 -)
Turn right side out and place the hot water bottle inside.

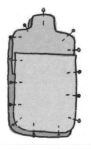

8

2

4

TIP

➤ Add a couple of drops
of lavender oil when the
scent begins to fade.

Night owl lavender cushion

In folklore, pillows were filled with lavender to help the restless fall asleep. If you have trouble sleeping, perhaps one of these embroidered cushions made from vintage fabric will send you into a peaceful slumber.

Time needed: One hour

You will need:	Fabric scissors	Pins
Dried lavender	Iron and board	Rice
Fabric	Needle and thread	Straight pins

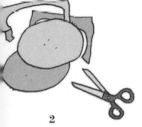

2

(- 1 -)
Prepare the filling by mixing **70 per cent dried lavender** with **30 per cent rice**. The rice helps to add weight to the cushion.

(- 2 -)
Cut two ovals of fabric a little larger than you want the finished cushion to be.

(- 3 -)
Handstitch the owl's features onto one piece.

(- 4 -)
Pin the front and back pieces together with the two right sides facing.

(- 5 -)
Stitch all around, using a 1cm (³⁄₈in) seam allowance and leaving a 2cm (³⁄₄in) gap.

(- 6 -)
Press the seam open.

(- 7 -)
Turn right side out and fill with the lavender-and-rice mixture.

(- 8 -)
Handstitch the opening closed.

3

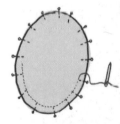

5

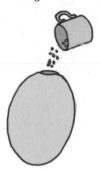

7

⟨ · BATHING · ⟩

Parisian shower curtain – **Scrap-wood bathtub caddy**
Twiggy towel ladder – **Handpainted towels** – **Crate cabinet**
Recycled toiletry bag – **Printing block toothbrush holder**

TIP
⟶ Use a lightweight fabric that will dry quickly.

Parisian shower curtain

Disguise an uninspiring shower curtain with a recycled, removable and washable cover.

Time needed: Two hours

You will need:

Fabric

Fabric scissors

Hammer

Iron and board

Measuring tape

Metal rivets

Needle and thread

Shower curtain

Straight pins

Tailor's chalk

· 1 ·

Take down your shower curtain and measure its size.

· 2 ·

Adding an extra 7cm (2¾in) to the length and 4cm (1½in) to the width of the shower curtain, cut out your fabric.

· 3 ·

Using a 2cm (¾in) hem allowance, fold, pin and press a hem at the bottom of the fabric.

· 4 ·

Repeat at the two sides.

· 5 ·

At the top, fold, pin and press a 5cm (2in) hem.

· 6 ·

Sew in place all around.

· 7 ·

Place the fabric right side down on the floor and lay the shower curtain, right side down, on top.

· 8 ·

Making sure the top two corners are aligned, mark the position of the rivet holes on the shower curtain onto the fabric.

· 9 ·

Make a small hole in the fabric where each mark is and, following the manufacturer's instructions, insert the rivets.

· 10 ·

Lay the fabric on top of the shower curtain, line up the rivets and rehang.

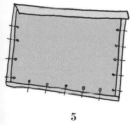

5

8

9

TIP

⇛ Use a non-toxic wood varnish to preserve the life of your caddy.

Scrap-wood bathtub caddy

If you have a rolltop bath (clawfoot bathtub), contrast sleek ceramic with rustic wood by adding a recycled bathtub caddy.

2

Time needed: Two hours

You will need:
Coping saw
Drill

Drill bit
Measuring tape
Pencil

Rounded file
Sandpaper
Screws

Wire
Wood

· 1 ·
Gather your wood. You need two pieces about 8cm (3¼ in) wide, 2cm (¾ in) thick and as long as the width of your bath. You also need enough wood about 5mm x 2.5cm (¼ x 1in) to make ten 15cm (6in) lengths.

· 2 ·
Measure the widest part of your bath and trim the two long pieces of wood to this size to form the rails of the caddy.

3

· 3 ·
Bend a small piece of wire snugly over the rim of the bath to make a template of the curve. Lay the rails in position across the bath and, using the wire as a guide, transfer the curve onto both ends of each rail with a pencil. Leave a 4cm (1½ in) gap between the top of the curve and the edge of the rail.

· 4 ·
Cut out the curves with the saw and test-fit them across the bath, making any necessary adjustments. File them in a nice smooth arc, finishing with sandpaper.

5

· 5 ·
Once they fit snugly, lay them across the bath and make a pencil mark underneath each end of both rails, 1cm (⅜ in) in from the side of the bath.

· 6 ·
Cut ten 15cm (6in) strips from the thin wood to make the slats, and sand them smooth.

· 7 ·
Drill a screw hole 1cm (⅜ in) from each end of two strips.

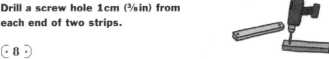

7

· 8 ·
Lay the rails upside down on a flat surface and place the two slats at each end next to the pencil marks and flush with the sides of the rails.

· 9 ·
Drill through the holes into the rails and screw the slats into place.

· 10 ·
Lay the remaining slats in place, space them evenly, and mark each one's position with a pencil.

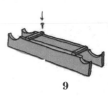

9

· 11 ·
Drill through the end of each slat into the rail, making sure they are still lined up with the marks.

· 12 ·
Screw all the slats into place.

Twiggy towel ladder

Celebrate well-worn timber with this rustic towel ladder made from driftwood.

Time needed: One hour

You will need:
Drill
Drill bit
Saw

Screws
Sandpaper
Well seasoned
driftwood

1

· 1 ·

Cut two pieces of driftwood 150cm (59in) long and four pieces 80cm (31½in) long.

· 2 ·

Paying attention to the irregular forms of the wood, lay the pieces on the floor to find the most pleasing arrangement.

· 3 ·

Make any necessary adjustments to the lengths of the pieces and sand the ends smooth.

3

· 4 ·

Lay the pieces on the floor again with the legs on top of the rungs.

· 5 ·

Drill through the legs where they cross the rungs and screw together.

· 6 ·

Sand the bottom of the legs into a dome so that they will not mark the floor and can lean at an angle.

5

6

TIP
➤ Instead of driftwood, try using well-seasoned timber with the bark removed. Add more rungs to make a longer ladder, if you like.

Handpainted towels

Transform tired towels with bold handpainted designs.

Time needed: One hour

You will need:

Fabric paints
Iron and board
Paintbrush
Tailor's chalk
Towels

(· 1 ·)
Wash and dry the towels to remove any dirt or chemical residue.

(· 2 ·)
Decide on your design and mark it out roughly on the towel with tailor's chalk.

(· 3 ·)
When you are happy with the design, follow the manufacturer's instructions to apply the paint.

(· 4 ·)
Fix the design according to the manufacturer's instructions.

(· 5 ·)
Wash and dry the towels before use to ensure that the paint is truly fixed.

1

2

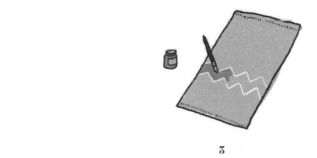

3

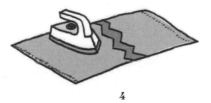

4

TIP
>>> Use graphic spots and stripes for a contemporary look.

Crate cabinet

Hide away essential but unsightly bathroom supplies
in this simple cabinet constructed from a disused pallet.

Time needed: Two hours

You will need:
Hammer
Measuring tape
Nails

Pencil
Sandpaper
Saw
Wooden pallet

4

· 1 ·
Dismantle the pallet and choose pieces
for the doors, top, sides and so on.

· 2 ·
Cut two lengths to form the vertical sides
of the box. These can be any size you like.

· 3 ·
Measure the width of these boards and
double it.

· 4 ·
Cut two lengths this size for the top and
bottom of the box. This ensures the panelling
for the back and the doors will fit neatly.

· 5 ·
Nail the four pieces together, placing the top
and bottom between the sides.

· 6 ·
Now measure the gap between top and
bottom and cut four lengths this size.

5

6

· 7 ·
Nail two of these in place to form a solid
wall of panelling across the back.

· 8 ·
The remaining two pieces of wood will form
the cabinet doors. Sand one long edge on
each door until it is well rounded. This will
give them clearance to open.

· 9 ·
Drill 1.5cm (⅝in) holes at the other side
of each door to make finger pull handles.

· 10 ·
Slot the doors into place and hammer
round nails through the top and bottom
of the cabinet and into the doors to
form hinges.

· 11 ·
If you want to add a shelf, cut a piece
to fit across snugly and nail into place.

8

10

TIP
→ Use oilcloth or another waterproof fabric for a wipe-clean bag.

Recycled toiletry bag

These bags are easy to make out of old fabric and make great
gifts for friends. Use them for toiletries and cosmetics
or as pencilcases and purses instead.

Time needed: One hour

You will need:

Fabric	Marker pen	Pinking shears
Fabric scissors	Measuring tape	Straight pins
Iron and board	Needle and thread	Zipper 16cm (6in) long
	Paper	

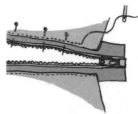

10

· 1 ·

Make a pattern by taking a piece of paper
25 x 20cm (10 x 8in) and folding it in half.

· 2 ·

Cut a square 3 x 3cm (1¼ x 1¼in) out of
each bottom corner.

· 3 ·

Mark 2.5cm (1in) in from the two top
corners and draw a diagonal line from each
mark towards the outer corner of the
cutaway square. Cut this triangle away.

· 4 ·

When open, the pattern should look
like illustration number 4.

· 5 ·

Lay the pattern on the fabric, pin together
and cut out. Repeat to give yourself a piece
of lining fabric.

· 6 ·

Lay the fabric right side down and place
the lining fabric on top.

· 7 ·

Fold one straight raw edge over by 1cm
(⅜in). Press.

· 8 ·

Pin the zipper to this edge and stitch
it in place.

· 9 ·

Mark where the two fabric ends will meet
and open the zipper.

· 10 ·

Fold down and press the other raw edge,
pin the zipper in place and sew.

· 11 ·

Turn wrong side out and, with the zipper
half open, sew along the diagonal edges,
1cm (⅜in) in from the edge.

· 12 ·

Press the seams open and trim any
excess with pinking shears.

· 13 ·

Now pinch together the bottom corners
and sew a straight line at each corner to
seal the bag. Again, trim any excess with
pinking shears.

· 14 ·

Turn right side out.

11

13

Printing block toothbrush holder

Give new life to old printing blocks by upcycling them into monogrammed toothbrush holders.

Time needed: 15 minutes

You will need:
Drill
Drill bit
Pencil
Ruler
Toothbrush
Wooden printing block

1

2

· 1 ·
Using a pencil and ruler, make marks at the centre of the top and bottom surfaces of the block.

· 2 ·
Drilling into the mark on top of the block, make the first hole with a drill bit slightly larger than the thickness of your toothbrush's handle. Be careful to drill as vertically as possible to ensure you don't go through the side.

· 3 ·
Depending on the shape of your toothbrush, you will probably need to drill holes on either side of the first one to make a large enough slot.

· 4 ·
Once the toothbrush fits in easily, drill a single hole through the mark on the bottom to join up with the existing holes. This allows water to drain through the block.

3

4

⊏ – DINING – ⊐

Tea-stained tablecloth – Vintage placemats – Handpainted china

Handprinted napkins – Newspaper napkin rings

Upcycled chair seat – Bunny tea and egg warmers

Tea-stained tablecloth

Tea-staining is a natural way to soften bright colours and give a warm, aged appearance to fabric. This tablecloth is simply made by dyeing bedlinen and lends a romantic feel to the dining room.

Time needed: One hour plus drying time

You will need:
Bath or bucket
Fabric

Teabags
Vinegar
Water

(1)
Wash the fabric to remove any dirt or chemical residue. Leave damp.

(2)
Fill a bath two-thirds full with hot water.

(3)
As the water is running, add teabags. The more tea you use, the stronger the colour will be. The tablecloth pictured here was dyed using 15 black teabags, but experiment to get different depths of colour.

(4)
Leave the bags to steep for ten minutes, then remove.

(5)
Add the damp fabric to the water, making sure it is fully immersed.

(6)
Leave to soak for 20 minutes, agitating regularly with your hands.

(7)
Remove the fabric from the bath and rinse it in a nearby sink with clean water.

(8)
Dry the fabric.

(9)
Fix the dye by soaking the fabric for ten minutes in a water/vinegar solution (1 teaspoon vinegar to 5 litres or 4½ quarts water). Rinse, then leave to dry.

8

9

3

5

Vintage placemats

Placemats make sitting down to dinner far more enjoyable.
These simple rectangles are made with leftover upholstery fabric,
but any other fabric would work just as well.

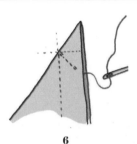

Time needed: One hour

You will need:
Fabric
Fabric scissors
Iron and board

Measuring tape
Needle and thread
Straight pins

7

⌐ 1 ⌐
Wash, dry and press the fabric before
you begin.

⌐ 2 ⌐
Cut out one piece of fabric 47 x 37cm
(18½ x 14½in) for each placemat. This
includes a 2cm (¾in) hem allowance
all around.

⌐ 3 ⌐
To prepare the hem, start by creating
mitred corners. These will help the placemat
lie flat. With the right side of the fabric
facing up, fold up the hem allowance all
round and press.

⌐ 4 ⌐
Unfold the hem allowance. Turn in one
corner at the point where the folds cross,
press, then open out again.

⌐ 5 ⌐
Fold the new crease in half, neatly lining up
the edges. You now have a triangular piece
of fabric.

⌐ 6 ⌐
Stitch along the crease shown, leaving 5mm
(¼in) at the end open. Backstitch both
ends of the stitching.

⌐ 7 ⌐
Snip off the triangle leaving 5mm (¼in)
and trim the point right up to the stitching.

⌐ 8 ⌐
Press the seam open.

⌐ 9 ⌐
Fold back and press the raw edge 5mm
(¼in) all the way around. Repeat on the
remaining three corners.

⌐ 10 ⌐
Turn inside out, press again, then pin
and stitch all around, 3mm (⅛in) inside
the hem.

9

10

Handpainted china

See the fluid forms of unwanted china in a new light
when transformed with specialist ceramic and glass paint.

Time needed: One hour plus drying time

You will need:
Ceramics
Ceramic and glassware
paints

Newspaper
Paintbrush

[- 1 -]

Choose unwanted ceramics with strong
silhouettes. Don't worry if they are
decorated with outdated patterns and
motifs, you will be covering these and
highlighting the form instead.

[- 2 -]

Wash and dry the ceramics.

[- 3 -]

Lay newspaper on a flat surface and sit the
pots on top.

[- 4 -]

Decide on your design and mix the paint
accordingly.

[- 5 -]

Follow the paint manufacturer's instructions
for application. Some brands need to be
fired in an oven, while others are simply left
for a few hours to dry.

[- 6 -]

Once complete, pots should be dishwasher-
safe and ready for use.

3

4

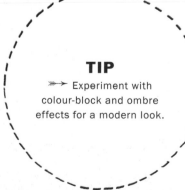

5

TIP

⫸ Experiment with
colour-block and ombre
effects for a modern look.

Handprinted napkins

Handprinting napkins is a great way to make use of old linen or cotton fabric.

Time needed: Two hours

You will need:

Fabric	Iron and board	Pencil
Fabric printing ink	Lino	Plate
Fabric scissors	Lino-cutting tools	Roller
	Needle and thread	Wooden spoon

6

⌐ 1 ⌐

Wash, dry and press the fabric before you begin.

⌐ 2 ⌐

For each napkin, cut a 52 x 52cm (20½ x 20½in) square of fabric.

2

⌐ 3 ⌐

Cut a piece of lino and draw your design onto it. Simple shapes work best, as fine details will not show up on most fabrics.

⌐ 4 ⌐

When you are happy with your design, carve around it carefully with the lino-cutting tools. Trim the lino close to the edge of the design with a pair of scissors to remove any waste area that might print accidentally.

3

⌐ 5 ⌐

Lay the fabric right side up on a flat surface and choose your ink.

⌐ 6 ⌐

Pour the ink onto a plate until there is a good flat area of colour that can coat a roller thinly. If your block is small, you can press it into the colour directly; otherwise, place it on a flat surface and apply the ink with a roller to ensure even coverage.

⌐ 7 ⌐

Do a test print on a piece of scrap paper.

⌐ 8 ⌐

When you are happy with the print, repeat the process on your fabric, working across the fabric until it is covered. You will need to ink the block before every print. Use the back of a wooden spoon to apply even pressure to the printing block.

⌐ 9 ⌐

Fix the ink according to the manufacturer's instructions and leave to dry.

8

⌐ 10 ⌐

Finish the napkins by folding, pressing and stitching a 2cm (¾in) hem allowance on each side.

10

Newspaper napkin rings

Napkin rings don't need to be boring. This is a simple and lighthearted way to recycle yesterday's news.

Time needed: Two hours plus drying time

You will need:

Empty toilet paper rolls
Glue bowl
Glue brush
Newspaper
Paper scissors
PVA glue (all-purpose white glue)
Varnish
Water

(- 1 -)
Cut the toilet paper rolls into strips 4cm (1½in) wide.

(- 2 -)
Cut the newspaper into strips 2 x 8cm (¾ x 3¼in).

(- 3 -)
Pour the glue into a dish and water it down slightly. The ratio should be one part water to three parts glue.

(- 4 -)
Layer the newspaper onto the toilet paper roll by dipping a strip of paper in the glue then laying it onto the cardboard.

(- 5 -)
Continue until all the cardboard is covered, overlapping as you go. Build up layers of newspaper, making sure that the pieces lay flat without any bubbling.

(- 6 -)
When you have applied five layers, leave to dry overnight.

(- 7 -)
Coat with varnish to seal and allow to dry.

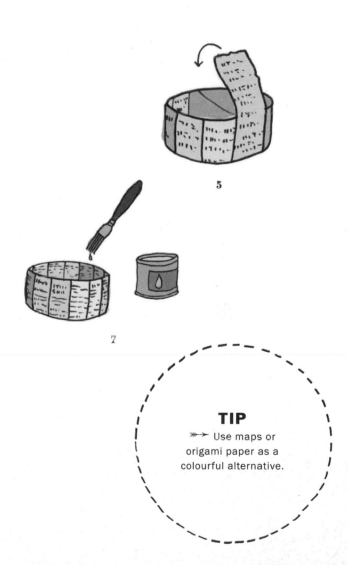

TIP
Use maps or origami paper as a colourful alternative.

Upcycled chair seat

This woven dining chair was inspired by Natalie Chanin's Friendship Chairs in her book, *Alabama Studio Style*. The simple method of weaving a fabric seat is a great way to upcycle unwanted textiles and give new life to an unused chair.

Time needed: Two hours

You will need:
Bodkin
Chair
Fabric
Fabric scissors

6

1

3

4

- 1 -
Prepare your chair by removing the old seat and making sure the area is clean and dry. If you want to sand or paint the chair, this is the time to do it.

- 2 -
Cut fabric into long strips 4cm (1½in) wide and sort into piles by colour. This chair was woven using old T-shirts, but you could use any strong fabric.

- 3 -
Create the warp threads by tying strips of fabric around the front of the seat and pulling them taut, stretching to the back. Knot securely with a double knot at the bottom of both ends. Leave a tail of fabric hanging down for decoration if you wish. Make sure the strips are pulled taut, as this will strengthen the seat.

- 4 -
Continue this process until the entire seat is covered.

- 5 -
Begin weaving the weft by tying strips to the left side of the seat and threading the end through a bodkin.

- 6 -
Weave under and over the warp threads, pulling taut and knotting in place on the opposite side.

- 7 -
Continue until the whole seat is complete.

TIP

⟫ Weave different coloured stripes for variety.

Bunny tea and egg warmers

Tea and egg cosies are a fun way to brighten up the breakfast table. These cute rabbit-shaped cosies are made from leftover handmade wool felt and require very little stitching.

Time needed: Two hours

You will need:

Fabric
Fabric scissors
Iron and board
Needle and thread

Paper
Paper scissors
Pen
Photocopier
Straight pins

2

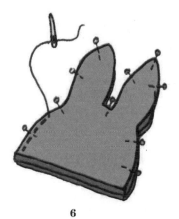

(- 1 -)
Photocopy the templates provided (see next page) and increase or decrease the size to fit your teapot and eggcups as necessary.

(- 2 -)
Cut out the templates.

(- 3 -)
Press the fabric.

(- 4 -)
Pin two pieces of fabric together.

(- 5 -)
Pin the template onto the fabric and cut out, creating the front and back pieces.

(- 6 -)
Pin and stitch together either by hand or machine. Leave the bottom edge raw.

5

6

TIP

≫ Highlight your stitching with contrasting thread.

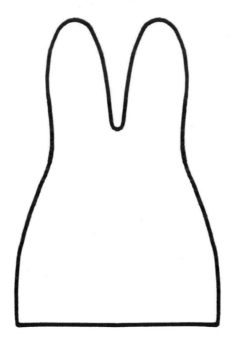

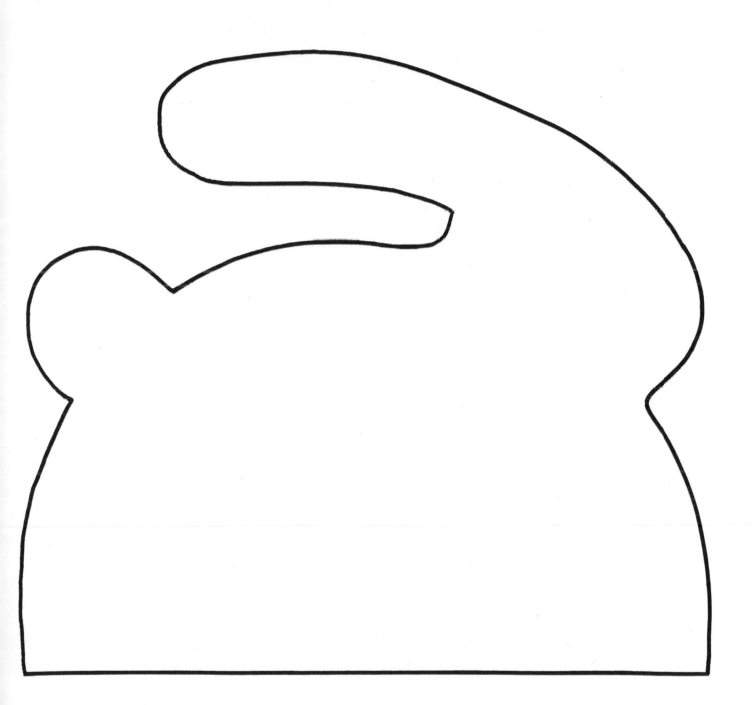

[· UTILITY ·]

Shaker peg rail - **Flat out ironing board cover**
Reworked peg bag - **Potato-printed tea towels** - **Reused oven mitt**
Handknitted dishcloths - **Recycled bag dispenser**

TIP
≫→ Try using sturdy twigs instead of dowelling.

Shaker peg rail

This Shaker-inspired peg rail made from scrap wood creates useful and stylish hanging space.

Time needed: Two hours

You will need:

Dowelling	Paint
Drill	Paintbrush
Drill bit	Pencil
Measuring tape	Wood
	Wood glue

1

3

5

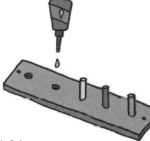

9

[· 1 ·]

Measure how long you want your peg rail to be. Pegs should be 15cm (6in) apart with 10cm (4in) between each end peg and the end of the rail. So cut your wooden plank to a length that is a multiple of 15cm (6in) plus 20cm (8in).

[· 2 ·]

Sand both ends smooth with sandpaper.

[· 3 ·]

Make a mark with a pencil 10cm (4in) in from each end and draw a light pencil line between them along the centre of the board.

[· 4 ·]

Divide the space between these marks into 15cm (6in) sections and mark where each peg will go.

[· 5 ·]

Drill holes either vertically or at an angle as deep as possible without going through the back of the wood.

[· 6 ·]

On the reverse side, drill 4mm (³⁄₁₆in) holes 3cm (1¼in) in from each end for wall mounting.

[· 7 ·]

Chop the dowelling into lengths of around 10cm (4in) and sand the ends smooth.

[· 8 ·]

Paint the pegs with leftover paint or tester pots and leave to dry.

[· 9 ·]

Glue the pegs into the holes and leave to dry overnight.

Flat out ironing board cover

Make ironing more enjoyable with a pretty ironing board cover.

Time needed: Two hours

You will need:
Bias binding (bias tape)
Fabric
Fabric scissors
Needle and thread

Old ironing board cover
(to use as a pattern)
Paper
Paper scissors
Sticky tape

Straight pins
String
Tape measure

· 1 ·
Join pieces of paper with sticky tape until you have a sheet as large as your old ironing board cover. Flatten the old cover, lay it on the paper and draw around it, adding an extra 4cm (1½in) all round. Cut out the pattern.

· 2 ·
Lay the fabric on a flat surface, wrong side facing up. Pin the pattern to it and cut the fabric out. Unpin.

· 3 ·
Take the bias binding and turn over the short edge by 2cm (¾in). Press in place.

· 4 ·
Starting at the middle of the flat short edge of the fabric, pin one fold of the bias binding onto the right side of the fabric. Leave the other side of the binding loose.

· 5 ·
Pin all the way around. When you reach the start point, overlap the binding by 2cm (¾in) and cut.

· 6 ·
Turn over the second short edge by 2cm (¾in) and pin in place so that they meet neatly.

· 7 ·
Stitch the binding to the fabric where pinned, using a 1cm (⅜in) seam allowance.

· 8 ·
Turn the fabric over so that the wrong side is facing up.

· 9 ·
Lay the string along the centre of the binding (leave a tail of a few centimetres).

· 10 ·
Turn down and stitch the loose edge of the binding, tucking in the string within the binding 'channel' as you go. Continue all the way around.

· 11 ·
Cut off any remaining string, leaving a tail of 6–8cm (2½–3¼in).

· 12 ·
Pull the two string ends to gather the cover's edges. Lay onto your ironing board, over the foam padding and pull tight. Tie the string edges into a neat bow.

1

4

7

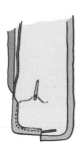

10

Reworked peg bag

A line of washing blowing in the breeze is a beautiful sight. Air-drying is not only economical and environmentally friendly, it also takes gentle care of clothes, making them last longer. A bag will keep your clothes pegs (clothespins) in order.

Time needed: 30 minutes

You will need:
Fabric
Fabric scissors
Iron and board
Measuring tape
Needle and thread
Straight coat hanger with clips
Straight pins

7

· 1 ·
Remove the clips from the coat hanger.

· 2 ·
Cut a square piece of fabric, 5cm (2in) wider than your coat hanger, and cut another piece the same width but 10cm (4in) longer.

2

· 3 ·
Make a straight cut across the second piece about three-quarters of the way up.

· 4 ·
Fold, press and pin a 1cm (⅜in) hem along one side of the square piece, both long sides of the small piece, and one long side of the remaining piece.

4

· 5 ·
Stitch the hems neatly.

· 6 ·
Place the large piece on a flat surface right side up with the hemmed edge at the top.

· 7 ·
Lay the small piece on top of this, right side down, lining up the hemmed edges, before laying on the other piece right side down and lining up the raw edges along the bottom.

· 8 ·
Pin together and sew around the edges, rounding the corners off slightly and allowing 1cm (⅜in) either side of the width of the coat hanger. Leave a 2cm (¾in) gap at the top to pass the hook through.

8

· 9 ·
Press the seams open and trim off any excess fabric with pinking shears. Turn right side out and insert the coat hanger.

9

Potato-printed tea towels

Create stylish tea towels (dish towels) with simple potato prints on recycled linen.

Time needed: Two hours

You will need:
Fabric
Fabric printing inks
Fabric scissors
Iron and board
Lino-cutting tools
or a sharp knife
Measuring tape
Needle and thread
Paper
Plate
Potatoes

· 1 ·
Wash, dry and press the fabric.

· 2 ·
For each tea towel, cut a piece of fabric 48 x 70cm (19 x 27½in).

· 3 ·
Slice a potato in half and create a printing block by cutting out your design with lino tools or a knife. Simple, bold designs work best.

· 4 ·
Mix the fabric ink on a plate and stamp the potato block into it. Alternatively, rub the ink into the block with your finger for a smooth result.

· 5 ·
Do some test prints on scrap paper to ensure the block is printing well. For an even result, press the block down firmly and wiggle it slightly.

· 6 ·
Lay the fabric right side up on a solid flat surface and print, reinking the block with each use.

· 7 ·
Once the ink is dry, fix according to the manufacturer's instructions.

· 8 ·
Sew a 1cm (⅜in) hem all around the edge of the fabric and press.

6

8

3

4

Reused oven mitt

Oven gloves get tired and greasy with constant use. Make
a new mitt from recycled fabric by following these easy steps.

Time needed: One hour

You will need:

Batting for insulation	Fabric	Marker pen	Paper scissors
Bias binding (bias tape)	Fabric scissors	Needle and thread	Rotary cutter
Cutting mat	Iron and board	Old oven mitt	Straight pins
	Lining fabric	Paper	

1

· 1 ·

To make a pattern, lay the old oven mitt on
a piece of paper and draw around it, adding
an extra 2cm (¾in) all around. Cut out.

· 2 ·

Cut two 28 x 36cm (11 x 14in) pieces
each from the main fabric, lining fabric
and the batting.

· 3 ·

Iron all six 28 x 36cm (11 x 14in) pieces.

· 4 ·

Make two sandwiches, each with one piece
of batting laid between the outer fabric and
the lining. Make sure the outer fabric is
facing out and pin together.

4

· 5 ·

With their right sides facing, lay the two
sandwiches of fabric together and pin.

· 6 ·

Place the pattern piece on top of the stack
and draw all around it with a marker pen.

· 7 ·

Following your marker lines, straight stitch
all around the oven mitt.

· 8 ·

Now cut out the mitt, cutting around
the stitching, leaving an extra 2cm (¾in)
all around.

· 9 ·

Clip into the seam allowance every 2cm
(¾in), being careful not to cut the stitching.

· 10 ·

Turn right side out.

7

· 11 ·

Trim the raw edges at the wrist of the
glove with a rotary cutter to make sure
they all line up neatly.

· 12 ·

Fold the bias binding in half lengthways
and press.

· 13 ·

Starting at one of the seams at the cuff of
the glove, pin the bias binding all around.
Tuck both short ends under neatly, to hide
the start and finish of the tape.

13

· 14 ·

Sew the bias binding in place, making
sure you catch the top and bottom as
you go.

Handknitted dishcloths

Made using recycled yarns, these handknitted dishcloths transform a simple necessity into a luxury.

Time needed: 30 minutes

You will need:
4mm (US size 6) knitting needles
Hand-sewing needle
Measuring tape
Scissors
Yarn

· 1 ·
Cast on 50 stitches.

· 2 ·
Garter stitch (every row knit) until work measures 20cm (8in).

· 3 ·
Cast off loosely.

· 4 ·
Cut and sew in loose yarn.

1

2

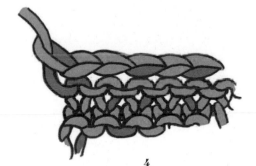

4

TIP
⟫→ Knit with string for a more abrasive dishcloth.

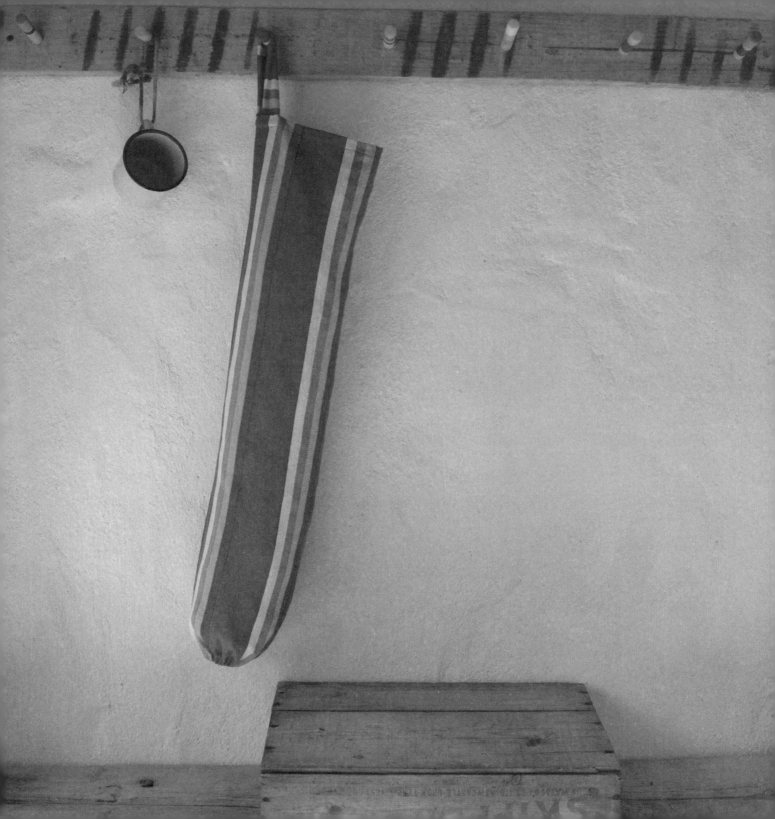

Recycled bag dispenser

Saving plastic bags for reuse often results in a mountain of bags. This easy bag dispenser will help you control your collection.

Time needed: One hour

You will need:

1cm (⅜in) elastic
Fabric
Fabric scissors

Iron and board
Loop turner (optional)
Measuring tape
Needle and thread

Safety pin
Straight pins

· 1 ·

Cut a 45 x 75cm (17¾ x 29½in) rectangle of fabric. Press.

· 2 ·

With the right side facing down, fold, press and pin a 2cm (¾in) hem along one of the 45cm (17¾in) sides. Don't sew yet.

· 3 ·

At the opposite end, fold, press and pin a 3cm (1¼in) hem.

· 4 ·

Attach the safety pin to one end of the elastic and thread through the 3cm (1¼in) hem. Be careful that the elastic does not twist.

· 5 ·

Sew the elastic in where it comes out at the end, 1cm (⅜in) in from the edge. Trim any excess elastic.

· 6 ·

Bunch the fabric towards the edge just sewn, to about half the unstretched width. Sew in the other side of the elastic and trim.

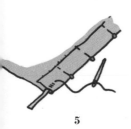

4

5

· 7 ·

Turn the fabric right sides together. Pin and stitch the long edge, including the top hem, which will need to be unfolded.

· 8 ·

Turn right way out. Fold in along the crease created in step 2. Topstitch around the outside, catching the edge around the inside.

· 9 ·

Make a looped handle by cutting a 7 x 30cm (2¾ x 12in) piece of fabric, folding in half with right sides together, and stitching. Turn inside out with a loop turner or your thumbs and press again. Alternatively, use a piece of ribbon.

· 10 ·

Stitch the loop in place at the back of the dispenser.

7

10

⊟ ← KIDS →⊟

Log cabin blanket - Ragbag bunting

Patchwork play mat - Newspaper bird mobile

Liberty suitcase - Mushroom rattle

TIP

⟩⟩⟩ Grow the blanket gradually by adding more blocks.

Log cabin blanket

This blanket is an appropriation of log cabin patchwork quilts. Traditionally, the central square of each block represents the fire in the home and the adjacent pieces symbolize day and night. Knitted with remnants of yarn rather than being made of scraps of fabric, the blanket brings a new twist to a traditional technique.

Time needed: A few months; this is a project to linger over and make a little at a time.

You will need:
4mm (US size 6) knitting needles
DK (double knitting/ worsted-weight) yarn
Hand-sewing needle
Iron and board
Scissors

5

3

The blanket is made up of 25 knitted blocks.

Each block contains a combination of pieces A, B, C and D.
A = 11 stitches, knit 16 rows
B = 22 stitches, knit 16 rows
C = 33 stitches, knit 16 rows
D = 44 stitches, knit 16 rows

(← 1 →)
Using 4mm needles and DK (worsted-weight) yarn, knit pieces in garter stitch (every row knit). You will need between 25 and 50 As; between 25 and 75 Bs; 50 Cs; and 25 Ds.

(← 2 →)
When you cast off, leave a long length of yarn for sewing up later.

(← 3 →)
To join together one block, overstitch all A and B pieces together, followed by C1, C2 and finally D.

(← 4 →)
Press flat when one block is sewn together.

(← 5 →)
When you have completed all 25 blocks, stitch together to create a 5 by 5 block blanket.

(← 6 →)
Sew in any loose ends and press.

Ragbag bunting

Use up small scraps of fabric to make this playful bunting.

Time needed: Two to three hours

You will need:
Fabric
Fabric scissors
Iron and board
Measuring tape
Needle and thread
Ribbon or cotton tape

2

Sort through your ragbag to select appropriate fabrics. This bunting is made with plain and patterned silks, but you could choose all cottons, jerseys, or even a mix of different fabrics instead.

Press the fabrics and cut them into strips 2 x 10cm (¾ x 4in). There is no need to be overly precise. Variation will make the bunting appear more lively. You could also cut traditional triangle shapes.

3

Fold the ribbon or tape in half vertically and press a crease along the fold.

Tuck each fabric swatch into the fold and pin in place.

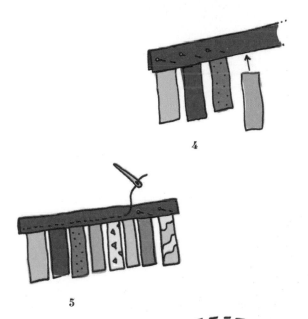

4

5

Stitch along the length of the ribbon, securing each piece of fabric in place.

Patchwork play mat

This mat is inspired by the quilts of Gee's Bend, a community of quilters based in Alabama, USA, making randomly patched quilts from recycled clothing and textiles. It is the perfect size for a play mat and is the ideal beginner's patchwork project.

Time needed: Four hours

You will need:
Batting
Cutting mat
Fabric

Fabric scissors
Iron and board
Measuring tape
Needle and thread

Rotary cutter
Ruler
Sewing machine
Straight pins

⟨← 1 →⟩
Select several pieces of contrasting cotton fabric. This is good for using up your scraps, so throw old cotton dresses and shirts into the mix.

⟨← 2 →⟩
Wash, dry and press the fabrics before you begin.

⟨← 3 →⟩
Cut out four pieces 80 x 25cm (31½ x 10in) and one piece 95 x 20cm (37½ x 8in).

⟨← 4 →⟩
With right sides facing, pin the 80 x 25cm (31½ x 10in) rectangles together along their long edges. Sew together with a seam allowance of 1cm (⅜in).

⟨← 5 →⟩
With right sides facing, pin the long edge of the 95 x 20cm (37½ x 8in) piece across the top of the four other pieces. Sew together with a seam allowance of 1cm (⅜in).

⟨← 6 →⟩
Sew in any loose ends and press.

4

⟨← 7 →⟩
Trim the seam allowance and press open.

⟨← 8 →⟩
Cut a piece of backing fabric 96 x 96cm (38 x 38in) and a piece of batting 96 x 96cm (38 x 38in).

⟨← 9 →⟩
With the patchwork piece laying wrong side up, make a sandwich by laying the batting on top of the patchwork and the backing fabric on top of the batting.

9

⟨← 10 →⟩
With a rotary cutter and ruler, neaten all the edges to the same length.

⟨← 11 →⟩
Pin around the edges and machine-stitch around the entire mat, using a 1cm (⅜in) seam allowance.

⟨← 12 →⟩
To make the binding, cut various pieces of fabric 12cm (4¾in) wide by any length, and sew together with a 1cm (⅜in) seam allowance along their short edges.

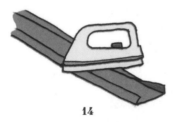

14

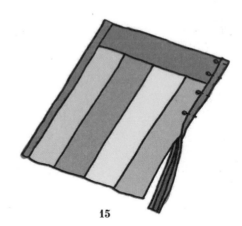

15

⟨← 13 →⟩

Trim the seam allowances and press open.

⟨← 14 →⟩

With the wrong side facing up, fold the two long edges in 2cm (¾in) towards the centre of the fabric. Press in place.

⟨← 15 →⟩

Pin the binding, wrong side to right side of mat, to the two opposite sides of the mat.

⟨← 16 →⟩

Repeat with the other two sides.

⟨← 17 →⟩

Machine-stitch in place, making sure to catch the top and bottom of the binding as you go.

⟨← 18 →⟩

To finish, quilt the mat with decorative embroidery stitches.

TIP

⟶ Don't want birds? Make a fish- or weather-inspired mobile instead.

Newspaper bird mobile

Entertain your little one with this pretty bird mobile made from newspaper scraps.

Time needed: 30 minutes

You will need:

Card
Coat hanger or wire
Glue stick
Hole punch
Newspaper
Paper scissors
Pencil
Pliers
Thread
Tracing paper

10

← 1 →
Transfer the bird template provided (see next page) onto card with tracing paper, or make your own.

← 2 →
Cut out the bird and use it as a template to cut four more birds from card.

← 3 →
Repeat this process with the wing shape, but using newspaper instead of card. Continue until you have five pairs of newspaper wings.

← 4 →
Use a hole punch to create an eye on each bird.

← 5 →
Cut six 20cm (8in) lengths of thread.

← 6 →
Spread glue on the tip of each wing and attach one to each bird, sandwiching the end of a piece of thread in between. Wings can be attached pointing either up or down for variation.

2

6

← 7 →
Glue the second wing to the opposite side of each bird.

← 8 →
Leave to dry, then fold each wing out gently.

← 9 →
Cut a piece of wire 25cm (10in) long and another piece 35cm (13¾in) long.

← 10 →
Roll each piece of wire around a pencil to create loops at each end.

← 11 →
Assemble the mobile by tying a bird with thread to each end loop, and one to the centre of the shorter wire. Vary the lengths a little and trim off any excess.

← 12 →
Attach extra thread to join the wires together, and at the top for hanging.

11

Liberty suitcase

When Liberty of London produced a limited-edition range of suitcases covered in their iconic floral prints, they sold out immediately. Make your own version by following the instructions below.

Time needed: Three hours

You will need:

Cardboard suitcase	Fabric	Pliers
Cloth	Fabric glue spray	Ruler
Coarse sandpaper	Fabric scissors	Tailor's chalk
Craft knife or scalpel	Masking tape	
	Measuring tape	

‹ 1 ›

Rub the suitcase all over with coarse sandpaper, then clean with a damp cloth. Leave to dry.

‹ 2 ›

Remove or mask off any hardware and remove the handle with pliers.

‹ 3 ›

Start by measuring the bottom half of the suitcase's exterior. Measure the length and add two times the depth plus an extra 5cm (2in). Measure the width and add two times the depth, plus an extra 5cm (2in) again. Cut a piece of fabric to this size.

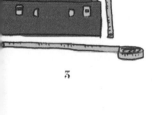

3

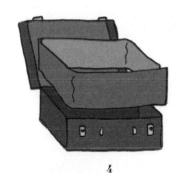

4

‹ 4 ›

Cut a piece of fabric to cover the interior four sides of the bottom of the suitcase.

‹ 5 ›

Cut a piece of fabric to neatly fit the base.

‹ 6 ›

Now measure the lid in the same way as in step 3, but add four times the depth as well as the extra 5cm (2in). Cut a piece of fabric to this size.

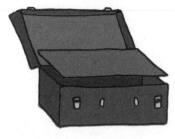

5

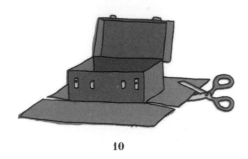

10

TIP

⋙→ A floral fabric helps disguise joins and creates a neat-looking finish.

⟨← 7 →⟩

Finally, cut a piece of fabric to fit neatly on the inside of the lid.

⟨← 8 →⟩

Press the fabric pieces.

⟨← 9 →⟩

Following the manufacturer's instructions, use the glue to stick the fabric cut in step 3 to the outside bottom of the case without pressing it onto the sides. Make sure there is an equal amount of fabric hanging over the front and sides, and smooth out any wrinkles as you go.

⟨← 10 →⟩

Make a cut in each corner and press the fabric onto the case, forming a neat overlap. Make any necessary snips to fit the fabric around the hardware.

⟨← 11 →⟩

Glue the fabric cut in step 4 around the inside of the base.

⟨← 12 →⟩

Now glue the fabric from step 5 into the base, smoothing any creases as you go.

⟨← 13 →⟩

Following the same technique, glue the pieces cut in steps 6 and 7 onto the lid. Leave to dry.

⟨← 14 →⟩

With a sharp craft knife or scalpel, neatly cut the excess fabric from around the hardware and remove the exposed masking tape.

⟨← 15 →⟩

Replace the handle.

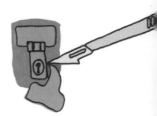

14

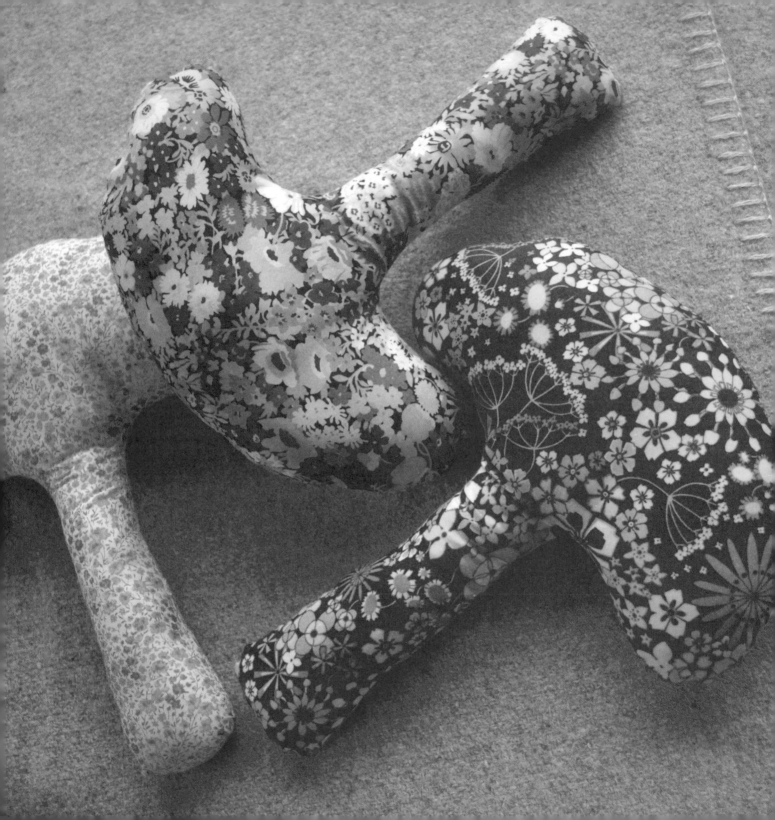

Mushroom rattle

Babies will love this mushroom rattle. Made from recycled fabric, it looks good enough to eat!

Time needed: 30 minutes

You will need:

Fabric	Marker pen	Small bell
Fabric scissors	Needle and thread	Straight pins
Iron and board	Paper	Stuffing
	Paper scissors	

3

⊰ 1 ⊱

Wash, dry and press the fabric before you begin.

⊰ 2 ⊱

Make a pattern by drawing a mushroom on a piece of paper. Make it a little larger than you want the actual rattle to be. The height should be about 20cm (8in) and the widest point about 15cm (6in). Alternatively, use figure 3 and increase the size on a photocopier. Cut out the pattern.

⊰ 3 ⊱

Fold the fabric. Pin the pattern to the fabric and cut out two mushroom shapes.

4

⊰ 4 ⊱

If you want to embroider a face or any other decoration on the rattle, do so now.

⊰ 5 ⊱

Lay the two pieces of fabric right sides together and pin. Stitch all around the edge, leaving the bottom unstitched.

⊰ 6 ⊱

Press the seam open.

⊰ 7 ⊱

Turn right side out.

5

⊰ 8 ⊱

Fill with stuffing and a small bell. Keep filling until the rattle is well padded.

⊰ 9 ⊱

Fold under the opening, pin closed and slipstitch the gap closed by hand.

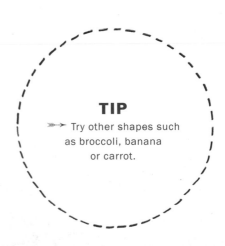

8

TIP

⋙ Try other shapes such as broccoli, banana or carrot.

⊂·Ξ OUTDOOR Ξ·⊃

**New old deckchair - Scrap-wood window box
Salvaged café chairs - Recycled bird house - Tribal teepee**

New old deckchair

Whiling away the afternoon in a deckchair is one of the joys of summer, but most vintage deckchairs come with dangerously perished seats. Thankfully, renovating them with new covers is a quick and easy task.

Time needed: One hour

You will need:
Deckchair
Fabric scissors
Hammer
Iron and board

Measuring tape
Needle and thread
Paint (optional)
Pliers
Sandpaper

Straight pins
Strong fabric such as deckchair canvas
Upholstery tacks

6

1

4

⟨ 1 ⟩
Looking at how the canvas is attached, use pliers to remove the old fabric and any nails/pins holding it in place.

⟨ 2 ⟩
Lightly sand the wooden frame and paint if desired.

⟨ 3 ⟩
Use the old seat as a guide for the new fabric. Cut a new piece of fabric the same length as the old one but 4cm (1½in) wider.

⟨ 4 ⟩
Using a 2cm (¾in) allowance, fold, press and pin a hem on each side.

⟨ 5 ⟩
Stitch securely.

⟨ 6 ⟩
Starting at the bottom of the chair, wrap the fabric, right side up, around the front rail.

⟨ 7 ⟩
Secure in place behind the rail with upholstery tacks, spaced 10cm (4in) apart.

⟨ 8 ⟩
Bring the fabric up towards the top of the chair and repeat, wrapping the fabric around the rail and securing in place with upholstery tacks.

7

TIP

⟫➤ Spinach, rocket (arugula), endive and radicchio can all be grown as cut-and-come-again varieties. Save money with packets of mixed seed.

LETTUCE

Scrap-wood window box

Use an old wooden pallet to create a home for herbs, flowers or salad leaves on your windowsill.

Time needed: Two hours

You will need:

Hammer
Measuring tape
Nails
Pencil
Sandpaper
Saw
Wooden pallet

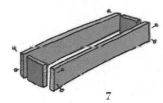

7

⟨⊷ 1 ⊶⟩
Measure the length of your windowsill and determine what size you want the window box to be.

⟨⊷ 2 ⊶⟩
Dismantle the pallet and choose three pieces of wood of equal width, long enough to form the base and sides of the window box.

⟨⊷ 3 ⊶⟩
Mark your desired length onto two pieces of wood and saw them to size.

⟨⊷ 4 ⊶⟩
Smooth both boards with sandpaper.

⟨⊷ 5 ⊶⟩
Make two end pieces by cutting two square pieces of wood the same size as the width of the board.

⟨⊷ 6 ⊶⟩
Sand these pieces.

⟨⊷ 7 ⊶⟩
Nail the two end pieces between the two long pieces. Place them with the cut edges hidden. This will make the box neater and more weatherproof. Skew the nails by hammering them in at opposing angles to make the joints stronger.

⟨⊷ 8 ⊶⟩
Drill pilot holes for nails if the wood is splitting easily.

⟨⊷ 9 ⊶⟩
Measure the gap lengthwise between the two ends and cut a final board to form the bottom of the box. This should slot in neatly and can be nailed in place.

5

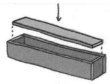

9

TIP

≫ > A sharp, good-quality
drill bit will make
a cleaner hole.

Salvaged café chairs

Worn-out café chairs can be given a new lease of life by replacing damaged and broken slats.

Time needed: One hour

You will need:		
Café chair	Measuring tape	Saw
Drill	Paint or varnish	Scrap wood
Drill bit	(optional)	15mm (⅝in) screws
Hacksaw	Pencil	
	Sandpaper	

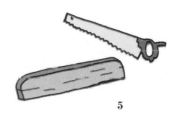

5

⟨← 1 →⟩
Remove any old slats by sawing them across the middle and levering them off so they break.

⟨← 2 →⟩
Cut off the bolts with the hacksaw to leave a flat surface for the new slats.

2

⟨← 3 →⟩
If you are lucky, the bottom of the old bolts will fall out. If not, you will need to drill new holes as close to them as you can. Make sure the holes are wide enough to fit the new screws.

⟨← 4 →⟩
Cut two strips of wood to go across the back and four or five for the seat. These should overhang the frame of the chair by 2cm (¾in) on each side.

⟨← 5 →⟩
Cut the edges off the front slat to leave rounded corners and sand all the pieces smooth.

3

⟨← 6 →⟩
Paint or varnish the slats if you wish.

⟨← 7 →⟩
Lay the slats in position on the chair and mark their positions underneath, through the bolt holes, using a pencil.

⟨← 8 →⟩
Drill pilot holes through the pencil marks without going through the other side.

⟨← 9 →⟩
Replace the slats on the chair and fix them into place through the holes with the screws.

7

Recycled bird house

Encourage birds to nest in your garden with a handmade bird house or box, made from scrap wood.

Time needed: One hour

You will need:

Drill	Hook	Ruler
Drill bit	Measuring tape	Sandpaper
Flat file	Nails	Saw
Hammer	Paint for outdoor use	Scrap wood
	Pencil	Set square (drafting triangle)

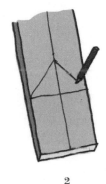

2

4

5

(← 1 →)

These houses are made out of a length of 2 x 15cm (¾ x 6in) plank, but different widths would work just as well.

(← 2 →)

Mark the shape of the gables in pencil by drawing a line down the centre of the plank to make sure the diagonals are equal sizes. The gables can be any size or proportion you wish.

(← 3 →)

Cut out the gables with a saw, then drill a 3cm (1¼in) diameter door hole in one of them.

(← 4 →)

For the sides, cut two pieces the same height as the verticals on the gables and cut down the width of each one by 3cm (1¼in).

(← 5 →)

Nail the sides between the gables, making sure all edges are aligned neatly.

(← 6 →)

Measure the space at the bottom and cut a piece to fit in and form a floor. Nail this into position.

(← 7 →)

To make the roof, sit the house on its base on a flat surface and lay a piece of wood on top so it overhangs the side by a few centimetres or couple of inches and is flush with the front gable.

(← 8 →)

Place the set square on the flat surface, running through the apex of the gable, and mark a vertical line in pencil on the edge of the roof piece.

(← 9 →)

Use the set square to continue this line all around the roof piece, then saw through this mark.

(← 10 →)

Cut another identical piece and test-fit them on the roof. Use the flat file to make any necessary adjustments to the angle of the cuts.

(← 11 →)

Once they fit tightly, with no leaky gap, nail them into place so they are overhanging a little on all sides.

(← 12 →)

Sand, paint and screw a hook into the bird house for hanging.

8

9

TIP
⟫⟶ This teepee is big enough for two adults. Adjust the measurements to make a bigger one.

Tribal teepee

This teepee makes a great garden (or beach) hideout for grown-ups, kids or animals.

Time needed: Two hours

You will need:

Fabric
Fabric paint
Fabric scissors
Iron and board
Knife
Marker pen or pencil
Measuring tape
Needle and thread
String
Rivets
Tent pegs
Wooden poles

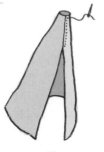

(- 1 -)
You will need six poles at least 250cm (99in) long. They can be made from any long, straight wood. Remove any bark from the poles for a smooth finish.

(- 2 -)
Using a knife, taper one end of each pole so that they can be pushed into soft ground.

(- 3 -)
The cover can be made up of canvas, tarpaulin or bedsheets sewn together, but you need enough to make a semicircle with a 200cm (79in) radius.

(- 4 -)
Press the fabric.

(- 5 -)
Lay the fabric out flat and mark out the semicircle using a pen and 200cm (79in) of string as a compass.

(- 6 -)
Mark an 8cm (3¼in) radius circle from the same point. (You may need to make this larger depending on the size of the poles.)

5

7

(- 7 -)
Cut out the shape and hem all rough edges.

(- 8 -)
Insert rivets every 50cm (20in) around the bottom edge.

(- 9 -)
Paint a design on the side to personalize your teepee. Follow the manufacturer's instructions.

(- 10 -)
Stitch the straight edges together at the top for 50cm (20in) to create a small round hole.

(- 11 -)
Measure 200cm (79in) along the poles and fasten them together at this point by wrapping the string around several times and knotting securely.

(- 12 -)
Pass the poles through the hole, pull them apart where they stick out at the top, and stand the whole structure upright, forcing the tapered ends into the ground. Put tent pegs through the rivets to secure the fabric to the ground.

10

11

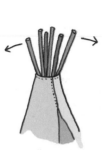

12

Glossary

ABUTTED SEAM Seam used to join two pieces of fabric edge to edge. Generally used to join interfacing and interlining to eliminate bulk.

BASTE A long stitch that will later be removed.

BATTING Cotton or synthetic wadding.

BIAS Diagonal line on fabric. The 'true' bias is the diagonal line formed at a 45-degree angle when the lengthways grain is folded to the crossways grain.

BIAS BINDING (BIAS TAPE) Strips available ready-made, cut on the bias grain of fabric; used to neaten edges.

BIAS BINDING MAKER Tool used to create bias binding by folding and pressing a fabric strip.

BINDING Method of finishing a raw edge by enclosing it in a strip of fabric. Also a notion; e.g., bias binding or ribbon. Used for practical purposes such as neatening a raw edge or strengthening a seam.

BLINDSTITCH Handstitch used for hemming and finishing, invisible on the right side of an item. Also, a zigzag machine stitch.

BODKIN Thick-bodied needle with a blunt end and large eye, used to thread elastic, tape or cord through a casing or heading.

CASING Tunnel of fabric through which elastic or drawstring cord is threaded.

CAST ON Make the first row of stitches when knitting.

CAST OFF Make the last row of stitches when knitting.

CLIP Small cut in fabric. Seam allowances and corners are often clipped to create a sharp point when turned to the right side.

COPING SAW Saw with a very narrow blade stretched across a U-shaped frame, used for cutting curves in wood.

CREASE Line formed from a pressed fold.

CROSSWAYS FOLD Widthwise folding of fabric made at the cutting stage.

CUTTING MAT Rubber mat with a grid design for precise measuring and cutting; used to protect a work surface during fabric or card cutting.

DOWEL A solid cylindrical rod, usually made of wood, plastic or metal.

FLAT FILE A metalworking and woodworking tool used to cut fine amounts of material from a work piece.

GARTER STITCH Every row knit.

GRAINLINE Line that follows the grain of a fabric.

HEADING Fabric tuck above a casing, or at the top edge of a curtain or blind.

HEADING TAPE Fabric tape containing loops that is stitched to the top of a curtain for the insertion of hooks.

HABERDASHERY (NOTIONS) Sewing accessories such as buttons, zips, thread and trimmings.

HEM Edge of a piece of cloth or clothing that has been turned under and sewn.

HEM ALLOWANCE Amount of fabric allowed for turning under to make up a hem.

JERSEY Knitted, crease-resistant, cotton fabric.

LAWN Fine cotton fabric.

LAYERING Trimming of fabric layers at a seam allowance to different widths to remove bulk.

LENGTHWAYS GRAIN Direction of the lengthways (warp) threads on a woven fabric, which runs parellel to the selvedges. As it is less likely to stretch than the crossways grain, the lengthways grain is used as the straight grain wherever possible.

LINEN Produced from the natural fibres of the flax plant, linen fabric is cool and highly absorbent.

LINING Underlying fabric layer used to give a luxurious, neat finish, as well as providing structural support and concealing details of construction.

MITRE BOX Hand tool for guiding handsaws in making crosscuts or mitre joints.

MITRED CORNER Diagonal seam formed when fabric is joined at or shaped around a corner (e.g. where the hems meet in the corner of a square).

NEEDLE GRABBER Sewing aid with a textured surface, used during handstitching to pull a needle through thick or unyielding fabric.

OVERLOCKING Quick and efficient stitching, trimming and edging of fabric in a single action.

OVERSTITCH Stitch made over an edge or over another stitch.

PANEL PIN Light slender nail with a narrow head.

PILOT HOLE Small hole drilled into a piece of wood to prevent it from splitting when it receives a screw or nail.

PINKING SHEARS Cutting tool with serrated blades, used on fray-resistant fabrics to neaten a seam allowance with a zigzagged finish.

PRINTING BLOCK Block on which a design for printing is engraved.

PVA GLUE (ALL-PURPOSE WHITE GLUE) Water-based non-toxic adhesive suitable for paper, wood, cardboard and textiles.

RAW EDGE Cut fabric edge.

REVERSE STITCHING Straight machine stitch that is worked backwards at the beginning and end of a seam to secure the threads before cutting off.

RIGHT SIDE Outer side of a fabric, designed to appear as the visible part of a finished item.

ROTARY CUTTER Tool with interchangeable round blades, used to create straight edges when cutting fabric. It should be used with a cutting mat.

RUNNING STITCH Handstitch used for seaming and gathering.

SANDPAPER Abrasive paper used for smoothing or polishing woodwork or other surfaces.

SEAM ALLOWANCE Extra fabric allowed on a pattern where pieces are to be joined together by a seam.

SEAM EDGE The cut edge of a seam allowance.

SEAM RIPPER Hooked cutting tool used to open and undo seams.

SEAMLINE Line designated for stitching a seam.

SELVEDGE (SELVAGE) Finished edge on a woven fabric, which runs parallel to the warp (lengthways) threads.

SET SQUARE (DRAFTING TRIANGLE) Tool used to provide a straight edge at a right angle.

SLIPSTITCH Handworked hemming stitch used to attach a folded fabric edge to another layer.

SPOT TACK To sew a few stitches in one spot, by hand or by machine, to secure one item to another.

STITCH-IN-THE-DITCH Short length of stitching used to create stability.

TACKING Long stitches made by hand or machine to hold fabric in position temporarily.

TAILOR'S CHALK Chalk used to mark fabric, removed by brushing.

THIMBLE Made of metal or plastic, this protective cap fits over a finger during handstitching, and aids in pushing a needle through unyielding fabric.

TIMBER Wood prepared for use in building and carpentry.

TOPSTITCHING Row of straight stitching worked on the right side of an item, close to the finished edge.

VICE Holding device attached to a workbench with two jaws to hold work firmly in place.

WARP Lengthways threads or yarns of woven fabric.

WEFT Threads or yarns that cross the warp of a woven fabric.

WEIGHT The measure of a fabric weight in grams per 100 square centimetres or ounces per square yard.

WRONG SIDE Reverse side of a fabric, which should be on the inside of a finished item.